Say It Now:
THANK YOU TO A TEACHER

Say It Now:
THANK YOU TO A TEACHER

A Teacher's Journal

Mindy Jo Sloan

BALBOA
PRESS
A DIVISION OF HAY HOUSE

Balboa Press books may be ordered through booksellers or by contacting:

Balboa Press
A Division of Hay House
1663 Liberty Drive
Bloomington, IN 47403
www.balboapress.com
1-(877) 407-4847

Because of the dynamic nature of the Internet, any web addresses or links contained in this book may have changed since publication and may no longer be valid. The views expressed in this work are solely those of the author and do not necessarily reflect the views of the publisher, and the publisher hereby disclaims any responsibility for them.

The author of this book does not dispense medical advice or prescribe the use of any technique as a form of treatment for physical, emotional, or medical problems without the advice of a physician, either directly or indirectly. The intent of the author is only to offer information of a general nature to help you in your quest for emotional and spiritual well-being. In the event you use any of the information in this book for yourself, which is your constitutional right, the author and the publisher assume no responsibility for your actions.

Any people depicted in stock imagery provided by Thinkstock are models, and such images are being used for illustrative purposes only.
Certain stock imagery © Thinkstock.

Printed in the United States of America

ISBN: 978-1-4525-6665-8 (sc)
ISBN: 978-1-4525-6666-5 (e)

Balboa Press rev. date: 1/30/2013

This book is dedicated to effective teachers everywhere.

ACKNOWLEDGEMENTS

Madison
Leah
Christopher
Kendall

INTRODUCTION

This is a book expressing appreciation and giving thanks to teachers. Why teachers? Because the contributions of an effective teacher benefit all of us.

If you are an effective teacher this book is meant for you. You are important. You can facilitate the development of healthy children who eventually become caring adults, and by doing so can help to create a better world.

Before a nurse, carpenter, accountant, minister, or architect, there must have been someone like you. So it makes sense to conclude that you are a valuable part of any community.

As one who has chosen to do this work you belong to a profession that impacts every child. Other than parenting, there are few professions that have as many opportunities as your own to develop tomorrow's adults. Your influence is not only directly expressed by each child, but eventually by the children of those students. It is a ripple effect that continues for generations and ultimately shapes society.

For this reason, you must be healthy. When you are emotionally and spiritually healthy, adequately prepared, and sufficiently supported your students benefit. When this is not the case, children are the first and most negatively impacted. If children matter, you must matter as well.

Effective teachers like you deserve a thank you. You deserve an opportunity to develop, refine, and utilize skills that promote self-examination, self-care, and ultimately self-improvement.

This journal not only says thank you, it provides a daily routine of self-care and self-exploration. Each day's section begins by saying thank you for a particular contribution. It is followed by a brief reflection on the day's events. You are asked to identify something learned each day. You are presented with an activity to increase self-knowledge. Each task encourages personal and unique expressions. The day ends with a self-affirmation so you understand your great value and personal worth.

Schools should be wonderful places to work, supplies should be bountiful, and for the purposes of this book most importantly, effective teachers like you should be recognized and respected for what you do for society, and our children most specifically.

THANK YOU . . .

This book contains 30 thank you messages just for you. Some messages describe the approaches of teachers such as you who interact well with students and parents, others recognize your professional skills, and the third group expresses thanks for all the extra time and energy you sacrifice. The thank you messages in this book do not begin to cover all of your contributions. Instead, they are meant to represent the general principle that effective teachers like you should be recognized and appreciated for what you do on a daily basis.

Consider the Day

It is important to take a moment and reflect on each day. You may want to look at what went well, and at what you want to do differently in the future. By reflecting on each day, it may be possible for you to better identify and define your feelings and behaviors. There is a tendency, particularly in the field of education, to focus upon deficits rather than strengths. In addition to looking at what you want to change, it is important to look at what is working and what you want to continue into the future. In doing this, you will become revitalized and learn to have greater appreciation for yourself. You will also find it easier to guide and teach others to have similar successes. As you know, it is important to teach learners what not to do, but it is even more important to teach them what to do. By helping yourself, you become a positive role model. And remember, you may be one of the only positive role models in the lives of some children.

Each message of thank you is followed by a brief request that you focus on the events of the current day. You are asked to rate the day on a scale of 1 to 10, with 1 being a very very challenging day and 10 being one of the most wonderful. You are asked to describe the best part of each day, even if the rating is only a 1. The best part of the day may at times be difficult to find or seem minor, but the assumption is that every day has at least one positive aspect to it. Lastly, you are asked to recall at least one thing learned each day. It is hoped you will take the opportunity to become aware of what has been learned from accomplishments as well as mistakes.

Adventure and Imagination

Each day you will be given an opportunity to complete an activity that may increase your self-knowledge. Increasing self-knowledge is a lifelong endeavor. Teachers who know themselves well are in a better position to understand students and their needs, than are teachers who lack self-knowledge. Effective teachers are aware of their own interests, passions, strengths, and weaknesses. They know when they are doing the right thing and when they are making mistakes. They have insight into their own motivations and the things in life that are likely to easily upset them. They also tend to know how to react to their own stresses, calm themselves, and most importantly, how to meet their own needs through rest and rejuvenation.

Your own self-knowledge can be increased by reflecting on past choices and desires. The daily activities will engage you in self-knowledge by offering opportunities to reflect in creative ways.

Self-Affirmation

Affirmations are simple statements that can reinforce a positive self-image. If they are repeated numerous times they can become part of your belief system. Positive affirmations do not negate the need to be critical and realistic about your weaknesses and mistakes, but they can remind you that despite everything, you are lovable. You need to value yourself and feel good about who you are at the most basic level. This allows you to teach students to value themselves as well. Valuing others is an essential characteristic of those in a healthy society.

Optional Activities

The daily activities are only suggestions. You may revise or substitute any of them with an alternate or additional routine. Ideally, you will build a daily routine involving personal quiet time just for your own reflection.

Personal Time

One version of quiet time may be referred to as a moment for reflection, attunement, balance, meditation, or prayer. What it is called is less important than what it involves and can do for you. The following describes one approach.

Identify a quiet, peaceful place that you enjoy. Consider lighting, temperature, and outside surroundings. If you are at work and have few options, do the best you can.

Arrange a comfortable seating arrangement that will allow you to relax, yet stay awake. This could be sitting on a firm chair, placement on the floor, or lying on pillows. Your back should be erect to facilitate clear breathing. Your shoulders should be able to relax.

You may sit with your hands to your side, on your knees, or in some way positioned so that palms are up and they are relaxed.

Take a moment to sit in this space.

Do a mental scan of your body to identify any discomfort and adjust accordingly.

There is no right or wrong way to position yourself. Find what works for you.

As you sit for a moment, notice your heart beat.

Gently take in a deep breath. You may imagine you are breathing in white light. Notice it enter your nostrils and then exit.

Try it again. This time notice how it travels from your nostrils into your face, and then into your head.

Hold the breath for a moment.

Again tune into your heart beat. Gently breathe out. You may breathe out your mouth, noticing how the breath leaves each part of your face and head as it exits.

Now repeat the process, but this time – think the word "Peace" as you inhale. As you see the breath or white light fill your face and head, see it bringing the word "Peace" throughout. Hold it for a moment.

As you gently exhale, think the word "Calm". Watch the word "Calm" leave your face and head as the breath or white light exit with it. See the letters of the word float on your breath or absorb in the white light as it moves.

This time – select words that work for you. Words such as "Healing", "Love", or "Patience" may be helpful to you. Some choose to think of a word the helps them let go as they breathe out. This could include "Tension", "Fear", or "Guilt". What matters is that the process is meaningful for you.

Let's take your breath into the rest of your body. Breathe in through your nostrils.

See the white light traveling down through the top of your head. It stops in your temples, then moves down into your cheeks and mouth. Slowly it moves to your spinal column, through your shoulders, and into your heart. Notice it spread throughout your chest.

From your chest it moves into your abdomen, then pelvic area and down through your legs. Notice how the light impacts parts of your body. As it enters a place where there is discomfort, imagine letting the pain dissolve into the light.

Gently begin the process of breathing out. Watch your breath exit each area of your body as you breathe out. If you see your breath as white light, ask that the white light remain in your body as your breath exits.

Continue the breath exercise 3 or more times.

Once settled, breathe normally using the same visualization.

Repeat this process quietly to yourself for a few minutes.

As you continue this practice, you will find it more desirable to sit for longer and longer periods of time. If you are pressed on time, understand that even 2 minutes can make a difference.

You can begin to integrate this practice throughout your day. If you feel stress approaching, watch the breath enter and exit your body. If you are about to enter a room that you predict will contain tension, take a moment to breathe before you enter. If you are in a meeting and feel the tension mounting, do the same. Once you have practiced this in solitaire, you will find it comes easily to you wherever you are.

One more note – it is common to have thoughts cross your mind during this quiet time. Gently move them to the side. Watch them exit your head. Then continue your visualization. Over time the numbers of these thoughts will diminish. The more of them that appear, the more likely it is that this practice will benefit you.

Your mind may allow you the awareness you need to monitor your body, but over time your heart may take the lead. You may begin to see your breath enter your body from a variety of places on your arms, torso, legs, and/or head. Surround yourself with the light. Carry it with you to protect and guide you through the day. Refer to it whenever you feel yourself drifting from a place of peace.

Again – what is important is that you find the practice that works for you.

Daily Requests and Setting Your Intent

It may be rewarding to make a simple request or set your intent as you begin each day. This request or statement of intent can be made early in the day during a quiet moment that occurs at about the same time. For example, most of us are alone when we drive to work or after we drop off our children at school. This can be a nice time to turn down the radio, put the phone aside, and focus on a daily request or make an affirmation. It can be simple, such as, "Lead me with love" or 'Today I will do what is highest and best." Like personal time for reflection, prayer, or meditation the purpose is to take an opportunity to create the experiences you want to have in your life. If this activity is repeated daily at the same time, it will eventually become a habit. Each time you are in the same situation, for example driving in your car, you may be reminded to make a daily request or set your intent. You can do the same thing before you go to bed or at any other time during your day. Pick a time that will help you create this helpful habit.

For more information and to join the online community, access www.leahfoundation.com.

THANK YOU

for starting each day fresh with every student.

Effective teachers are able to start every day with a positive approach towards each student. They do not give up hope or resign themselves to believing a student is doomed for failure based on prior experience. Effective teachers understand that a student's past behavior may predict his or her future behavior, but they also know it is a responsibility of the teacher to break the cycle. They intervene when negative behaviors occur and teach students appropriate behaviors when necessary. Children are resilient creatures. They have the ability to respond to interventions, to make new choices, and to grow. Thank you, Effective Teacher, for beginning again and again and again.

SELF-CARE TOOLS

Get comfortable and take a deep breath. Let it out. It is your turn to relax. When you feel ready, reflect on your day. What went really well today? What do you wish you could have changed? On a scale of 1 to 10, with 1 being a very challenging day and 10 being one of the best, rate your day. Then complete the following statements.

I give today a rating of ——————————.

The best part of today was ——————————.

Today I learned ——————————.

Journal your thoughts to the following. You may substitute or add other activities if you wish.

What is your favorite children's story? Think about what it is about the major character that appeals to you. To what extent do you identify with a character? Determine if there is a moral or message to the story. What can you learn about yourself by understanding what attracts you to this story? Consider what others may learn about you. Reflect and respond in your journal.

Repeat the following affirmation to yourself, *"I see new opportunities every day."*

Slowly say the first word. Pause. Say the next word, pause, and continue until you have completed the statement. Repeat the process at least 10 times. Say it to yourself or write the affirmation in your journal until it feels real and you believe what it says. You may want to repeat this affirmation over the following days or weeks.

THANK YOU

for protecting a learner's right to be different.

Effective teachers understand the great many ways that students can learn. There are students who respond well to visual information, and others who remember things better when they hear or do them. Some learners are challenged academically, while others seem to excel with little or no effort. Students may require support in one subject, such as reading, but can work without assistance in another, such as math. Others benefit from help in all academic areas. There are learners who have difficulty paying attention, some who have poor social skills, and others who are learning the English language. Students have a variety of talents and gifts. Some of these gifts and talents fit easily into the traditional classroom environment, while others, such as creativity, do not. Effective teachers value uniqueness and develop lessons that allow individual expression. They embrace the richness that differences in learning provide to all students. Thank you, Effective Teacher, for protecting individuality.

SELF-CARE TOOLS

Get comfortable and take a deep breath. Let it out. It is
your turn to relax. When you feel ready, reflect on your
day. What went really well today? What do you wish you
could have changed? On a scale of 1 to 10, with 1 being
a very challenging day and 10 being one of the best, rate
your day. Then complete the following statements.

I give today a rating of _____.

The best part of today was _____.

Today I learned _____.

Journal your thoughts to the following. You may
substitute or add other activities if you wish.

Pretend you have been given an opportunity to go back in
time and rename yourself. What name would you select
for yourself? Would you name yourself after someone
or invent a completely original name? Would it have a
specific meaning? Use your journal to describe the name
and why you picked it.

Repeat the following affirmation to yourself, *"I am (insert your new name)."*

Slowly say the first word. Pause. Say the next word, pause, and continue until you have completed the statement. Repeat the process at least 10 times. Say it to yourself or write the affirmation in your journal until it feels real and you believe what it says. You may want to repeat this affirmation over the following days or weeks.

THANK YOU

for sharing your lunch.

Many students, for a variety of reasons, come to school hungry. Studies indicate that a majority of learners who qualify for free or reduced lunch do not choose to consume these meals. And, some students are transported home via bus rides that last into the evening. All in all, there are a surprising number of children who are asked to learn on empty stomachs. Some teachers choose to share their lunches, others bring snacks to class, and still others have volunteers who contribute crackers, chips, or fruit to students as they study. Going beyond the call of duty, many effective teachers provide what they can to hungry students. Thank you, Effective Teacher, for filling stomachs as well as brains.

SELF-CARE TOOLS

Get comfortable and take a deep breath. Let it out. It is your turn to relax. When you feel ready, reflect on your day. What went really well today? What do you wish you could have changed? On a scale of 1 to 10, with 1 being a very challenging day and 10 being one of the best, rate your day. Then complete the following statements.

I give today a rating of _____.

The best part of today was _____.

Today I learned _____.

Journal your thoughts to the following. You may substitute or add other activities if you wish.

Pretend someone is bringing you your idea of the "perfect meal." To your delight, calories and nutrition are not factors in selecting items for this meal. What would it be? Explain the types of food and how it would be presented to you. Use your journal to describe this meal.

Repeat the following affirmation to yourself, *"I deserve good things."*

Slowly say the first word. Pause. Say the next word, pause, and continue until you have completed the statement. Repeat the process at least 10 times. Say it to yourself or write the affirmation in your journal until it feels real and you believe what it says. You may want to repeat this affirmation over the following days or weeks.

THANK YOU

for discovering each learner's interests.

Knowing students' interests allows an effective teacher to develop rewards that go beyond material objects, such as candy or stickers. For example, a student with an interest in motorcycles might be given an opportunity to use that topic in a presentation, research it online, or review relevant magazines. Knowledge of interests also allows one to better understand students and their unique backgrounds. It is helpful when teaching new information to present it in the context of knowledge that has already been gained. If a teacher knows what interests students, new information, put into the context of the interests, is much more likely to be learned. Effective teachers discover student interests so they can use it to improve learning. Thank you, Effective Teacher, for being interested in interests.

Self-Care Tools

Get comfortable and take a deep breath. Let it out. It is your turn to relax. When you feel ready, reflect on your day. What went really well today? What do you wish you could have changed? On a scale of 1 to 10, with 1 being a very challenging day and 10 being one of the best, rate your day. Then complete the following statements.

I give today a rating of _____.

The best part of today was _____.

Today I learned _____.

Journal your thoughts to the following. You may substitute or add other activities if you wish.

What would be worth missing sleep to see or do? Describe this experience in your journal.

Repeat the following affirmation to yourself, *"I do my best."*

Slowly say the first word. Pause. Say the next word, pause, and continue until you have completed the statement. Repeat the process at least 10 times. Say it to yourself or write the affirmation in your journal until it feels real and you believe what it says. You may want to repeat this affirmation over the following days or weeks.

Day 5

Thank you

for saying kind words to a child who
does not hear them often enough.

Not every student is given an opportunity to hear positive
comments, such as, "I enjoyed reading your paper." or
"Your calculations show a lot of hard work." Unfortunately,
some children hear nothing but criticisms and negative
remarks in their home lives, and even at school. Effective
teachers understand how destructive criticism can be.
They know how, and choose, to deliver kind words in
ways that elevate a child's self-image and hopes for
the future. One method is to make sure compliments
recognize effort, are very specific, and contain detail.
Saying, "Good job," is nice, but saying, "Your work shows
you know a lot about whales," is even better. Thank you,
Effective Teacher, for lifting up your students.

Day 5

Self-Care Tools

Get comfortable and take a deep breath. Let it out. It is your turn to relax. When you feel ready, reflect on your day. What went really well today? What do you wish you could have changed? On a scale of 1 to 10, with 1 being a very challenging day and 10 being one of the best, rate your day. Then complete the following statements.

I give today a rating of _____.

The best part of today was _____.

Today I learned _____.

Journal your thoughts to the following. You may substitute or add other activities if you wish.

Create a message of empowerment for a specific person who could benefit from it. What would the message include? Why would you give this message to this person? Respond in your journal. To what extent does your message empower you?

Repeat the following affirmation to yourself, *"I am powerful."*

Slowly say the first word. Pause. Say the next word, pause, and continue until you have completed the statement. Repeat the process at least 10 times. Say it to yourself or write the affirmation in your journal until it feels real and you believe what it says. You may want to repeat this affirmation over the following days or weeks.

THANK YOU

for showing compassion towards the angry child.

Many teachers report increasing numbers of angry children in the classroom. This anger, they report, interferes with learning and often leads to violent acting out. Effective teachers understand that anger may be an expression of sadness. That it may mask negative images towards self, frustration, and feelings of helplessness. Many students are not in touch with their own pain and lack the skills necessary to express it appropriately. Effective teachers know this. They see the angry child as a potential victim of his or her own lack of skills.

Understanding anger does not mean excusing its harmful expression. Firm consequences for negative behaviors are important. Effective teachers are not tolerant of aggressive behavior. However, they are successful in separating judgment of a behavior from judgment of the child. They can hate the behavior but love the child. Students who are met with unconditional positive regard from a teacher are more likely to respond well than those who are met with contempt and hostility. With the support of an effective teacher, students can be shown alternative methods for expressing negative emotions. Thank you, Effective Teacher, for responding to anger with love.

SELF-CARE TOOLS

Get comfortable and take a deep breath. Let it out. It is your turn to relax. When you feel ready, reflect on your day. What went really well today? What do you wish you could have changed? On a scale of 1 to 10, with 1 being a very challenging day and 10 being one of the best, rate your day. Then complete the following statements.

I give today a rating of _____.

The best part of today was _____.

Today I learned _____.

Journal your thoughts to the following. You may substitute or add other activities if you wish.

When do you feel loved by someone? Consider what convinces you that someone loves you. Describe loving behavior. How do you react? Reflect in your journal. What would someone learn about you by reading your response?

Repeat the following affirmation to yourself, *"I am lovable."*

Slowly say the first word. Pause. Say the next word, pause, and continue until you have completed the statement. Repeat the process at least 10 times. Say it to yourself or write the affirmation in your journal until it feels real and you believe what it says. You may want to repeat this affirmation over the following days or weeks.

THANK YOU

for spending your own money on school supplies.

It shouldn't happen, but it does. Many teachers spend their own money on school supplies. Schools don't usually provide consumable school supplies to students, and many learners don't come to class prepared. It is not unusual to find a teacher who at some point has brought in extra paper and pencils, markers, scissors, glue, or facial tissues to compensate for what is not available to learners. There has been an increased emphasis on relying less on traditional textbooks and supplementing lessons with activities. Activities often require additional supplies. Some teachers choose to spend their own money to buy interesting specialty books, arts and craft materials, or computer programs, for example. Individualizing lessons for learners with exceptionalities may involve specialized school supplies and result in teachers covering the costs of these materials as well. Thank you, Effective Teacher, for caring more about student learning than your bank account.

SELF-CARE TOOLS

Get comfortable and take a deep breath. Let it out. It is your turn to relax. When you feel ready, reflect on your day. What went really well today? What do you wish you could have changed? On a scale of 1 to 10, with 1 being a very challenging day and 10 being one of the best, rate your day. Then complete the following statements.

I give today a rating of _____.

The best part of today was _____.

Today I learned _____.

Journal your thoughts to the following. You may substitute or add other activities if you wish.

If you could have an endless supply of something, what would it be? Describe what you would do with it. Respond in your journal.

Repeat the following affirmation to yourself, *"There is an abundance of good in my life."*

Slowly say the first word. Pause. Say the next word, pause, and continue until you have completed the statement. Repeat the process at least 10 times. Say it to yourself or write the affirmation in your journal until it feels real and you believe what it says. You may want to repeat this affirmation over the following days or weeks.

Thank you

for balancing high expectations with reasonable goals.

Students should be challenged but not overwhelmed by school. It can be difficult to know how much work is too much work for learners, and when enough is not being expected. Effective teachers know how to require a level of work that brings out the most in each student. This can include consideration of the pace at which information is taught, the format and number of tests, and the complexity of materials. As an example, effective teachers consider homework in the context of each student's after school demands. For learners who work to help financially support their families, have significant domestic responsibilities, or function as primary caregivers, hours of homework each night are unreasonable. For those students who have an opportunity to focus primarily on academics, a demanding homework assignment each evening may be appropriate. Thank you, Effective Teacher, for setting the mark in the correct place for each student.

Self-Care Tools

Get comfortable and take a deep breath. Let it out. It is your turn to relax. When you feel ready, reflect on your day. What went really well today? What do you wish you could have changed? On a scale of 1 to 10, with 1 being a very challenging day and 10 being one of the best, rate your day. Then complete the following statements.

I give today a rating of _____.

The best part of today was _____.

Today I learned _____.

Journal your thoughts to the following. You may substitute or add other activities if you wish.

Imagine yourself as a line. What did you look like today?

Did you zigzag all around or run even and straight? Did you move uphill or head straight downhill? Were you going in circles? Use your journal to draw yourself as a line. With your finger, trace your line from beginning to end and reflect on your experiences along the way. Now, draw the type of line you want to be tomorrow or a year from now.

Repeat the following affirmation to yourself, *"I am special."*

Slowly say the first word. Pause. Say the next word, pause, and continue until you have completed the statement. Repeat the process at least 10 times. Say it to yourself or write the affirmation in your journal until it feels real and you believe what it says. You may want to repeat this affirmation over the following days or weeks.

DAY 9

THANK YOU

for creating an environment that supports learning.

Before students arrive at the beginning of a new school year, effective teachers are designing their classrooms to support learning. Seating arrangements for example, can be very important. Some learners perform better seated away from distractions such as windows or heating vents that come on and off during the day. Others benefit if seated in the front of the room or near the teacher. Group work is more manageable if desks are arranged to make tables, while individual work is easier if each desk is separated by space. A well lit, dry, and comfortable room is a prerequisite for performance. Procedures, such as lining up for lunch or getting up to sharpen a pencil, are much more likely to go smoothly if the room is arranged properly. It should be well organized and interesting enough to support learning without having too many distractions. Student work should be displayed year round. Other reference tools, such as the letters of the alphabet or the Periodic Table can be helpful if posted in a visible location. But too much on the walls can be overwhelming for some students. Thank you, Effective Teacher, for creating a classroom environment that is conducive to learning.

Day 9

Self-Care Tools

Get comfortable and take a deep breath. Let it out. It is your turn to relax. When you feel ready, reflect on your day. What went really well today? What do you wish you could have changed? On a scale of 1 to 10, with 1 being a very challenging day and 10 being one of the best, rate your day. Then complete the following statements.

I give today a rating of _____.

The best part of today was _____.

Today I learned _____.

Journal your thoughts to the following. You may substitute or add other activities if you wish.

Think about your favorite room in your home. What is it about this room that makes it special to you? What do you enjoy doing in it and what could someone learn by watching you in this room? Reflect and respond in your journal.

Repeat the following affirmation to yourself, *"I am valuable."*

Slowly say the first word. Pause. Say the next word, pause, and continue until you have completed the statement. Repeat the process at least 10 times. Say it to yourself or write the affirmation in your journal until it feels real and you believe what it says. You may want to repeat this affirmation over the following days or weeks.

THANK YOU

for attending to the "whole" child.

When people talk about eliminating barriers to learning they must consider a wide range of human needs. They must take into account emotional, physical, social, intellectual, and spiritual health. For teachers to really address learning, they too must be prepared to consider each student's needs in a very broad sense. Life is complicated for many learners, and if there are significant problems at home, learning will be difficult. Many times while working in collaboration with school psychologists, physicians, social workers, speech and language pathologists, and other professionals, effective teachers focus upon the "whole" child in the context of his or her unique background. Thank you, Effective Teacher, for understanding that there is more to students than their academic skills.

SELF-CARE TOOLS

Get comfortable and take a deep breath. Let it out. It is your turn to relax. When you feel ready, reflect on your day. What went really well today? What do you wish you could have changed? On a scale of 1 to 10, with 1 being a very challenging day and 10 being one of the best, rate your day. Then complete the following statements.

I give today a rating of _____.

The best part of today was _____.

Today I learned _____.

Journal your thoughts to the following. You may substitute or add other activities if you wish.

Reflect on the aspects of your family background that have had the greatest influences in your life. Are there things you say that you have heard older family members say? Do you do things that remind you of a relative? Consider the elements of your background that make you feel special and bring you joy. Describe your thoughts in your journal.

Repeat the following affirmation to yourself, *"I see my strengths."*

Slowly say the first word. Pause. Say the next word, pause, and continue until you have completed the statement. Repeat the process at least 10 times. Say it to yourself or write the affirmation in your journal until it feels real and you believe what it says. You may want to repeat this affirmation over the following days or weeks.

Day 11

Thank you

for taking risks and for teaching
students to do the same.

Learning can be a risky endeavor, particularly for those
who do not want to risk being wrong. Even the best
teachers don't always know the answers, and so good
teachers, like students, must be willing to say, "I made a
mistake" or "I don't know the answer." Effective teachers
encourage students to consider various possibilities
and to test new ideas. They reward learners for asking
questions. They encourage students to experiment a little,
hypothesize, and consider possibilities. Being wrong is a
necessary part of moving forward, and students will learn
to embrace this as the effective teacher appropriately
models this behavior in the classroom. Thank you,
Effective Teacher, for showing students that some risks
are worth taking.

Day 11

Self-Care Tools

Get comfortable and take a deep breath. Let it out. It is your turn to relax. When you feel ready, reflect on your day. What went really well today? What do you wish you could have changed? On a scale of 1 to 10, with 1 being a very challenging day and 10 being one of the best, rate your day. Then complete the following statements.

I give today a rating of ⎯⎯⎯⎯⎯⎯⎯⎯⎯⎯.

The best part of today was ⎯⎯⎯⎯⎯⎯⎯⎯⎯⎯.

Today I learned ⎯⎯⎯⎯⎯⎯⎯⎯⎯⎯⎯⎯.

Journal your thoughts to the following. You may substitute or add other activities if you wish.

What is your favorite piece of clothing? Do you have a comfortable pair of jeans, perfectly worn shoes, or fun hat? A shirt in the perfect color? Something you can wear anywhere and still look nice? A piece that has been washed a thousand times and still looks great? Use the journal pages to describe what you love about this piece of clothing. Explain how it makes you feel and any memories attached to it. What would someone learn about you by looking at your favorite piece of clothing?

Repeat the following affirmation to yourself, *"I am comfortable in my own skin."*

Slowly say the first word. Pause. Say the next word, pause, and continue until you have completed the statement. Repeat the process at least 10 times. Say it to yourself or write the affirmation in your journal until it feels real and you believe what it says. You may want to repeat this affirmation over the following days or weeks.

Thank you

for creating useful tools to assess student learning.

A significant amount of energy has been directed at big stakes testing in recent years. Big stakes testing tends to be initiated by national or state movements, and is directed at collecting group data to inform policy making decisions rather than compiling individual data that can be directly linked to creating instructional strategies for the classroom. Statewide and national testing does not take into consideration the individual needs and diversities of learners. Big stakes testing may have its place, but it does not serve the classroom teacher on a day-to-day basis. For assessment to be effective, measurement tools must be designed with the particular needs of individual learners in mind. Thank you, Effective Teacher, for creating assessment measures that are directly linked to relevant teaching strategies.

Day 12

Self-Care Tools

Get comfortable and take a deep breath. Let it out. It is your turn to relax. When you feel ready, reflect on your day. What went really well today? What do you wish you could have changed? On a scale of 1 to 10, with 1 being a very challenging day and 10 being one of the best, rate your day. Then complete the following statements.

I give today a rating of _____.

The best part of today was _____.

Today I learned _____.

Journal your thoughts to the following. You may substitute or add other activities if you wish.

Imagine you have the power to create one rule everyone in the world would follow. Describe the rule. Why did you select this rule? What would be the outcome of this rule? Reflect and describe in your journal.

Repeat the following affirmation to yourself, *"I am a good role model."*

Slowly say the first word. Pause. Say the next word, pause, and continue until you have completed the statement. Repeat the process at least 10 times. Say it to yourself or write the affirmation in your journal until it feels real and you believe what it says. You may want to repeat this affirmation over the following days or weeks.

DAY 13

THANK YOU

for giving the shy child needed time.

There are a variety of reasons students may seem shy or withdrawn. Sometimes there are cultural differences between learners and teachers, resulting in a misinterpretation of behavior as shy or withdrawn, when in fact the behavior may be, for example, a demonstration of respect. On the other hand, children who are fearful may appear shy. Learners who are new to a school, unique in some way, or experiencing difficulties at home may choose to withdraw in an attempt to protect themselves emotionally. Students who don't feel well, lack confidence, or have communication challenges may also appear shy. Under pressure, a shy student is likely to withdraw further or emotionally breakdown in class. Effective teachers may not immediately understand the cause for a behavior, but they do see the importance of giving a shy learner an opportunity to initiate contact or respond in his/her own time. They understand that only after feeling safe, is it likely a student will develop a relationship with and confide in a teacher so that support can be provided. Thank you, Effective Teacher, for drawing out the withdrawn student.

SELF-CARE TOOLS

Get comfortable and take a deep breath. Let it out. It is your turn to relax. When you feel ready, reflect on your day. What went really well today? What do you wish you could have changed? On a scale of 1 to 10, with 1 being a very challenging day and 10 being one of the best, rate your day. Then complete the following statements.

I give today a rating of _____.

The best part of today was _____.

Today I learned _____.

Journal your thoughts to the following. You may substitute or add other activities if you wish.

If no one would judge you, how would you wear your hair? Choose any color and style. Would you shave your head or let your hair grow wild? Describe what your hair would say about you. Reflect and respond in your journal.

Repeat the following affirmation to yourself, *"I am a miracle."*

Slowly say the first word. Pause. Say the next word, pause, and continue until you have completed the statement. Repeat the process at least 10 times. Say it to yourself or write the affirmation in your journal until it feels real and you believe what it says. You may want to repeat this affirmation over the following days or weeks.

THANK YOU

for showing each learner that school
is a place to succeed.

There should be an opportunity at school that allows every child to feel successful. Every child should look forward to going to school. But the reality is that many students don't like to go to school because they see it as a place of failure. For them, showing up at school each morning means they are reminded how little they know and how much they have to do to catch up. Their schoolwork is returned full of red ink and points taken off. Their names are written on a list and posted in the classroom to identify those who have not behaved well. Often they have a reputation as "trouble makers" or "slow learners". In response, some students accept the negative label and it becomes a self-fulfilling prophecy. They get good at making school a place to fail. Rather than strive for academic excellence, some students choose to define school as a place for "nerds" or "geeks" to succeed. Doing well in school is avoided. Because they feel rejected, they choose to reject the institution of education itself. Thank you, Effective Teacher, for showing students that school success belongs to everyone.

Day 14

Self-Care Tools

Get comfortable and take a deep breath. Let it out. It is your turn to relax. When you feel ready, reflect on your day. What went really well today? What do you wish you could have changed? On a scale of 1 to 10, with 1 being a very challenging day and 10 being one of the best, rate your day. Then complete the following statements.

I give today a rating of _____.

The best part of today was _____.

Today I learned _____.

Journal your thoughts to the following. You may substitute or add other activities if you wish.

Imagine someone is going to write a song to represent who you are. Think about what type of song it would be. Would it be rap, country, classical, pop, gospel, opera, or a show tune? To what extent would it have lyrics? Where would you like it played or sung? What instrument(s) would be involved? Describe your song in your journal.

Repeat the following affirmation to yourself, *"I am successful."*

Slowly say the first word. Pause. Say the next word, pause, and continue until you have completed the statement. Repeat the process at least 10 times. Say it to yourself or write the affirmation in your journal until it feels real and you believe what it says. You may want to repeat this affirmation over the following days or weeks.

DAY 15

THANK YOU

for seeing the many strengths of each student.

The field of education uses a deficit model to describe student learning. In other words, students are identified by academic deficit. Special education, services for at-risk learners, and support for English language learners are financially supported nationally and by individual states who seek to increase the academic performance of specific students. States may or may not choose to financially support students identified with particular talents. Describing students in terms of strengths is not as common as one would hope. Effective teachers however, articulate student strengths on a consistent basis. Every student, including those with academic needs, has strengths, according to an effective teacher. And those strengths can be used to overcome challenges or deficits in performance. Thank you, Effective Teacher, for first seeing what students can do, rather than what they cannot do.

Self-Care Tools

Get comfortable and take a deep breath. Let it out. It is your turn to relax. When you feel ready, reflect on your day. What went really well today? What do you wish you could have changed? On a scale of 1 to 10, with 1 being a very challenging day and 10 being one of the best, rate your day. Then complete the following statements.

I give today a rating of _____.

The best part of today was _____.

Today I learned _____.

Journal your thoughts to the following. You may substitute or add other activities if you wish.

Imagine you have won an award and are to be honored at an upcoming banquet. What would you want the award to demonstrate? What would you want it to say? Who would you want to give it to you? Describe your award in your journal.

Repeat the following affirmation to yourself, *"I find peace within myself."*

Slowly say the first word. Pause. Say the next word, pause, and continue until you have completed the statement. Repeat the process at least 10 times. Say it to yourself or write the affirmation in your journal until it feels real and you believe what it says. You may want to repeat this affirmation over the following days or weeks.

THANK YOU

for the nights you didn't sleep because you
couldn't stop thinking about the challenges
faced by one of your students.

There can be an emotional cost to effective teaching. It
involves caring about students. The same passion that
fuels a teacher's dedication can sometimes interfere with
his/her health. Maintaining appropriate boundaries is an
ongoing struggle, and even the best teachers sometimes
find they can't leave work at school. Thank you, Effective
Teacher, for risking your personal health in the name of
student learning.

Day 16

Self-Care Tools

Get comfortable and take a deep breath. Let it out. It is your turn to relax. When you feel ready, reflect on your day. What went really well today? What do you wish you could have changed? On a scale of 1 to 10, with 1 being a very challenging day and 10 being one of the best, rate your day. Then complete the following statements.

I give today a rating of _____.

The best part of today was _____.

Today I learned _____.

Journal your thoughts to the following. You may substitute or add other activities if you wish.

Get paper and pencil or pen in hand. You have 60 seconds to write as quickly as possible, as many things as you can that you are grateful for having in your life. Don't think about what you are writing, just write without judgment. After you have finished, reflect on your list. What surprises you?

Repeat the following affirmation to yourself, *"I have a rich life."*

Slowly say the first word. Pause. Say the next word, pause, and continue until you have completed the statement. Repeat the process at least 10 times. Say it to yourself or write the affirmation in your journal until it feels real and you believe what it says. You may want to repeat this affirmation over the following days or weeks.

THANK YOU

for opening the eyes of learners to a world of possibility.

For a variety of reasons many students do not have an awareness of the world in which they live. It has been reported that most learners are unable to identify states on a map or countries on a globe. Some have never been out of their immediate neighborhoods and don't consider opportunities that may exist for them in other places. Part of the task of a teacher is to expose students to the world and roles in life they may not have considered. Developing a personal dream can provide a student with a sense of direction and purpose. To do so requires the learner to establish long-term goals and align his/her behavior with attaining those goals. Not all students know how to dream of better things. They may have observed seemingly perfect lives on television or in movies, but creating their own is a concept they find foreign. Sometimes it helps to personally meet people who have found their dreams.

Guest speakers, such as the parents of learners, can provide examples of various lifestyles and talk about the education that was necessary to secure their jobs. Former graduates who return to their communities from other places can speak about their lives and what they feel is important to achieving success. Field trips are a useful tool in introducing ideas to students, and may include trips to college campuses. Effective teachers are willing to help all students see a world of possibilities. Thank you, Effective Teacher, for broadening students' horizons and dreaming with them.

Day 17

Self-Care Tools

Get comfortable and take a deep breath. Let it out. It is your turn to relax. When you feel ready, reflect on your day. What went really well today? What do you wish you could have changed? On a scale of 1 to 10, with 1 being a very challenging day and 10 being one of the best, rate your day. Then complete the following statements.

I give today a rating of _____.

The best part of today was _____.

Today I learned _____.

Journal your thoughts to the following. You may substitute or add other activities if you wish.

Some say the eyes are the windows to the soul. Look at one of your eyes in a mirror. What do you notice about it? Is there a perfect outlining ring? Identify each of its colors. Does its color change when you put other colors next to it? Does your eye change in the light? Look at the other eye. How alike or different are they? Consider what your eyes reveal about you. Reflect in your journal.

Repeat the following affirmation to yourself, *"I have insight."*

Slowly say the first word. Pause. Say the next word, pause, and continue until you have completed the statement. Repeat the process at least 10 times. Say it to yourself or write the affirmation in your journal until it feels real and you believe what it says. You may want to repeat this affirmation over the following days or weeks.

THANK YOU

for listening when you had many
other things to be doing.

Listening is a sure way of learning about someone. Effective teachers understand that students believe they are cared about when time is taken to let them be heard. Good listening involves direct eye contact, positioning one's body to face the person, responding with head movements, perhaps asking a short question or two, and paraphrasing back. Many times a teacher has to do very little other than listen to help a learner. Students can often solve their own problems simply by talking them through. But listening well takes time and that can be its biggest challenge, particularly when one is a classroom teacher with 30 or so other learners. Nevertheless, effective teachers see listening to students as an important responsibility and find a way to do it well. Thank you, Effective Teacher, for learning by listening.

Day 18

Self-Care Tools

Get comfortable and take a deep breath. Let it out. It is your turn to relax. When you feel ready, reflect on your day. What went really well today? What do you wish you could have changed? On a scale of 1 to 10, with 1 being a very challenging day and 10 being one of the best, rate your day. Then complete the following statements.

I give today a rating of _____.

The best part of today was _____.

Today I learned _____.

Journal your thoughts to the following. You may substitute or add other activities if you wish.

Imagine you have been given the ability to become invisible at will. Where would you go and what would you do with your talent? Decide how often you would choose to become invisible. Under what circumstances? What kinds of adventures would you consider? Use your journal to respond.

Repeat the following affirmation to yourself, *"I am a good observer."*

Slowly say the first word. Pause. Say the next word, pause, and continue until you have completed the statement. Repeat the process at least 10 times. Say it to yourself or write the affirmation in your journal until it feels real and you believe what it says. You may want to repeat this affirmation over the following days or weeks.

Day 19

Thank you

for staying up-to-date on the best teaching practices.

A significant amount of study has been directed at determining the best teaching practices for increased academic performance. An effective teacher understands that keeping up-to-date on the latest findings is an important responsibility. It involves being active in professional organizations, attending conferences and workshops, and reading educational journals. There is usually not time during a regular school day to pursue professional development. For this reason it occurs after school, on weekends, and during school breaks. Thank you, Effective Teacher, for staying current regarding new developments in the field of education.

DAY 19

SELF-CARE TOOLS

Get comfortable and take a deep breath. Let it out. It is your turn to relax. When you feel ready, reflect on your day. What went really well today? What do you wish you could have changed? On a scale of 1 to 10, with 1 being a very challenging day and 10 being one of the best, rate your day. Then complete the following statements.

I give today a rating of _____.

The best part of today was _____.

Today I learned _____.

Journal your thoughts to the following. You may substitute or add other activities if you wish.

Pretend you could not be a teacher. Identify another profession that you would go into. What would you like to do with your time and energy, if you could not teach? What would this second profession provide that is similar to or contrasts with what is provided to you by teaching? Reflect and describe your experience in your journal.

Repeat the following affirmation to yourself, *"I trust myself."*

Slowly say the first word. Pause. Say the next word, pause, and continue until you have completed the statement. Repeat the process at least 10 times. Say it to yourself or write the affirmation in your journal until it feels real and you believe what it says. You may want to repeat this affirmation over the following days or weeks.

DAY 20

THANK YOU

for reaching out to the loner student.

Resources have been directed at attempting to understand and predict school violence. School shootings are not confined to specific neighborhoods. They can happen anywhere, including middle class suburbs and affluent communities. After-the-fact investigations indicate that the shooters were typically troubled but often unnoticed prior to the violence. What seems common is that these troubled students did not feel they were accepted by the larger school community. They had not established positive relationships with peers or teachers and often preferred to be alone. Effective teachers reach out to these students so positive relationships can be established. If signs arise indicating that a serious problem may exist, involved teachers can notify appropriate people and steps can be taken to avoid potential violence. Thank you, Effective Teacher, for connecting with the disconnected.

DAY 20

SELF-CARE TOOLS

Get comfortable and take a deep breath. Let it out. It is your turn to relax. When you feel ready, reflect on your day. What went really well today? What do you wish you could have changed? On a scale of 1 to 10, with 1 being a very challenging day and 10 being one of the best, rate your day. Then complete the following statements.

I give today a rating of _____.

The best part of today was _____.

Today I learned _____.

Journal your thoughts to the following. You may substitute or add other activities if you wish.

If you could receive comfort in the arms of someone after a difficult day, who would that person be? What does this person provide that makes him/her your pick? Pretend this is happening and reflect on your feelings. Describe your experience in your journal.

Repeat the following affirmation to yourself, *"I lovingly embrace who I am."*

Slowly say the first word. Pause. Say the next word, pause, and continue until you have completed the statement. Repeat the process at least 10 times. Say it to yourself or write the affirmation in your journal until it feels real and you believe what it says. You may want to repeat this affirmation over the following days or weeks.

Thank you

for getting to school well before the sun has
risen and leaving well after it has set.

Once students arrive at school, there is little time to
prepare lessons, grade homework, design bulletin
boards, or contact parents. Some schools provide time
for teachers to plan during the week, but it may not be
enough. Effective teachers don't just teach students.
Good teaching requires preparation. There are materials
to review, lessons to be created, tests to be developed,
and copies to be made. Supplies must be collected, notes
to parents must be written, and rooms must be arranged.
Teachers are expected to attend faculty meetings and
participate on various work groups. They meet with
other school and community professionals to develop
individualized plans for students with exceptionalities.
Learners' experiences in the classroom are the end product
of a long list of lesser known teacher responsibilities.
Thank you, Effective Teacher, for investing the time
needed to do your job well.

Self-Care Tools

Get comfortable and take a deep breath. Let it out. It is your turn to relax. When you feel ready, reflect on your day. What went really well today? What do you wish you could have changed? On a scale of 1 to 10, with 1 being a very challenging day and 10 being one of the best, rate your day. Then complete the following statements.

I give today a rating of _____.

The best part of today was _____.

Today I learned _____.

Journal your thoughts to the following. You may substitute or add other activities if you wish.

Imagine you have won an opportunity to take the perfect vacation. Think about where you would go and how long you would stay. Would you travel around or remain in one place? Decide what you would do while you are there. Who might you take with you? Reflect and describe your perfect vacation in your journal. What could someone learn about you by reading your response?

Repeat the following affirmation to yourself, *"I am at peace."*

Slowly say the first word. Pause. Say the next word, pause, and continue until you have completed the statement. Repeat the process at least 10 times. Say it to yourself or write the affirmation in your journal until it feels real and you believe what it says. You may want to repeat this affirmation over the following days or weeks.

Day 22

Thank you

for embracing diverse points of view.

It is easier for a teacher to present information as factual than to open one's self to challenges from students. By opening one's self to diverse opinions on a topic, a teacher must accept the possibility that s/he could be wrong or simply not have an answer. Effective teachers don't feel the need to be all knowing, and are confident enough to embrace diverse points of view. They see themselves as lifelong learners and enjoy considering various opinions on a topic. They understand that diverse views may lead to discussions and learning opportunities that are not possible solely through their own lectures. Rather than perceive diversity as a threat, effective teachers recognize it as a strength. Effective teachers embrace diverse views understanding they may encourage students and teachers to reverse roles for a period of time, increasing knowledge for everyone. Thank you, Effective Teacher, for using diversity to benefit learners.

SELF-CARE TOOLS

Get comfortable and take a deep breath. Let it out. It is your turn to relax. When you feel ready, reflect on your day. What went really well today? What do you wish you could have changed? On a scale of 1 to 10, with 1 being a very challenging day and 10 being one of the best, rate your day. Then complete the following statements.

I give today a rating of _____.

The best part of today was _____.

Today I learned _____.

Journal your thoughts to the following. You may substitute or add other activities if you wish.

Imagine a door that has been closed to you in the past, has suddenly been opened to you. What is behind it? To what extent would you or your life change? Are you happy it is open? Respond in your journal.

Repeat the following affirmation to yourself, *"I am confident and capable."*

Slowly say the first word. Pause. Say the next word, pause, and continue until you have completed the statement. Repeat the process at least 10 times. Say it to yourself or write the affirmation in your journal until it feels real and you believe what it says. You may want to repeat this affirmation over the following days or weeks.

Thank you

for remembering how much loving parents
want their child to succeed.

As much as effective teachers care for their students, it doesn't compare to the love of nurturing parents for their children. No one wants a child to succeed more than does a loving parent or guardian. Knowing how interested these parents are in the success of their children, effective teachers choose to partner with them to provide the best services possible. Not every parent, however, has a positive perception of school. Many parents' perceptions of school are based on their own experiences as a student. If this experience was negative, parents may be intimidated, hesitant, or resistant to seeing a teacher as a partner in their child's academic success. Overcoming this obstacle requires the dedication and experience of an effective teacher. Thank you, Effective Teacher, for supporting loving parents.

SELF-CARE TOOLS

Get comfortable and take a deep breath. Let it out. It is your turn to relax. When you feel ready, reflect on your day. What went really well today? What do you wish you could have changed? On a scale of 1 to 10, with 1 being a very challenging day and 10 being one of the best, rate your day. Then complete the following statements.

I give today a rating of _____.

The best part of today was _____.

Today I learned _____.

Journal your thoughts to the following. You may substitute or add other activities if you wish.

Reflect on your reasons for initially becoming a teacher.

Remember why you chose to become a teacher. What did you hope to achieve? To what extent have your reasons for becoming a teacher changed? Take a moment to reflect, than respond in your journal.

Repeat the following affirmation to yourself, *"I am an effective teacher."*

Slowly say the first word. Pause. Say the next word, pause, and continue until you have completed the statement. Repeat the process at least 10 times. Say it to yourself or write the affirmation in your journal until it feels real and you believe what it says. You may want to repeat this affirmation over the following days or weeks.

THANK YOU

for preparing every student to be
tomorrow's caring adult.

Who do we want caring for us in our old age? We likely
want people who can read, write, add, subtract, who
understand history and politics, and who can use
technology. But we also want people who care about
humanity, contribute to the world around them, and take
personal responsibility. In partnerships with families
and communities, teachers can help guide children to
become the people the world needs. Thank you, Effective
Teacher, for helping to prepare the next generation to
make the world a better place.

SELF-CARE TOOLS

Get comfortable and take a deep breath. Let it out. It is your turn to relax. When you feel ready, reflect on your day. What went really well today? What do you wish you could have changed? On a scale of 1 to 10, with 1 being a very challenging day and 10 being one of the best, rate your day. Then complete the following statements.

I give today a rating of ＿＿＿＿＿＿＿＿＿＿.

The best part of today was ＿＿＿＿＿＿＿＿＿＿＿.

Today I learned ＿＿＿＿＿＿＿＿＿＿＿＿＿＿.

Journal your thoughts to the following. You may substitute or add other activities if you wish.

What is your very earliest childhood memory? Describe who it involves and what is happening in it. What was the setting? How do you fit into this memory? Reflect on how this memory has impacted your life over the years. Respond in your journal.

Repeat the following affirmation to yourself, *"I have faith in my abilities."*

Slowly say the first word. Pause. Say the next word, pause, and continue until you have completed the statement. Repeat the process at least 10 times. Say it to yourself or write the affirmation in your journal until it feels real and you believe what it says. You may want to repeat this affirmation over the following days or weeks.

THANK YOU

for grading homework when you'd rather be
spending time with family and friends.

It is Thanksgiving evening and the family is sitting around
the table playing a card game. The dedicated teacher,
however, is seated on the couch in the other room grading
papers. Sound familiar? Too often this is the case. It
would certainly be easier not to assign homework and
avoid the grading all together. Effective teachers however
don't consider this option. For them, student learning
is a high priority. And student learning increases with
detailed teacher feedback. Thank you, Effective Teacher,
for taking the time to provide constructive feedback.

SELF-CARE TOOLS

Get comfortable and take a deep breath. Let it out. It is your turn to relax. When you feel ready, reflect on your day. What went really well today? What do you wish you could have changed? On a scale of 1 to 10, with 1 being a very challenging day and 10 being one of the best, rate your day. Then complete the following statements.

I give today a rating of _____.

The best part of today was _____.

Today I learned _____.

Journal your thoughts to the following. You may substitute or add other activities if you wish.

If you could spend one entire day with someone, deceased or living, who would it be? Describe what you would spend the day doing. What would you ask or talk about? Reflect on what you would hope to gain. After responding in your journal, pretend that you had met this person and asked everything you had wanted to ask. What do you imagine you would have learned?

Repeat the following affirmation to yourself, *"I am creative."*

Slowly say the first word. Pause. Say the next word, pause, and continue until you have completed the statement. Repeat the process at least 10 times. Say it to yourself or write the affirmation in your journal until it feels real and you believe what it says. You may want to repeat this affirmation over the following days or weeks.

Day 26

Thank you

for paying attention to the child
who craves recognition.

Children who do not get the attention they need at home often try to get it at school. For these learners, any attention can be good attention. That is why effective teachers ignore negative behaviors whenever possible. They reward good behavior, and pay a minimal amount of attention to behaviors they want to eliminate. Students who want recognition quickly learn that pleasing behaviors are the way to be noticed. Thank you, Effective Teacher, for catching students being good.

Day 26

Self-Care Tools

Get comfortable and take a deep breath. Let it out. It is your turn to relax. When you feel ready, reflect on your day. What went really well today? What do you wish you could have changed? On a scale of 1 to 10, with 1 being a very challenging day and 10 being one of the best, rate your day. Then complete the following statements.

I give today a rating of _____.

The best part of today was _____.

Today I learned _____.

Journal your thoughts to the following. You may substitute or add other activities if you wish.

Pretend you have an incredible talent. What would it be and how would you use that talent? Write about this in your journal.

Repeat the following affirmation to yourself, *"I am talented."*

Slowly say the first word. Pause. Say the next word, pause, and continue until you have completed the statement. Repeat the process at least 10 times. Say it to yourself or write the affirmation in your journal until it feels real and you believe what it says. You may want to repeat this affirmation over the following days or weeks.

THANK YOU

for showing students how what is taught
in school relates to real life.

For students to feel motivated to expend energy on schoolwork, they often must be shown how it relates to their perceptions of real life. Effective teachers know how to link classroom tasks with real life by showing students what their lives would be like if they could not read, write, or add, for example. Imagine going to a restaurant and not knowing how to read the menu, not getting a driver's license because you couldn't navigate the written test, or not getting a job because you couldn't complete the application. What if you were never sure if you'd been given the correct change after a purchase? Math and science can make life seem more predictable, writing allows us to communicate without being present, history can teach us about the future, and reading supports us to keep learning over a lifetime. Effective teachers understand that doing well in school means more than learning specific pieces of information. It requires self-discipline, the ability to delay gratification, organization, and understanding how to find assistance when needed. It also means knowing how to learn in a fast paced, changing society. Effective teachers reward hard work in the classroom, expect organization and neatness, stress the importance of following rules and getting along with others, and role model good study skills. They also allow the learner to construct knowledge and develop the skills needed for lifelong learning. Linking classwork to real life means understanding each learner's "real life." Effective teachers take the necessary time and energy to familiarize themselves with students' individual lives and, thereby, define real life from the learner's perspective. Thank you, Effective Teacher, for making learning authentic.

Self-Care Tools

Get comfortable and take a deep breath. Let it out. It is your turn to relax. When you feel ready, reflect on your day. What went really well today? What do you wish you could have changed? On a scale of 1 to 10, with 1 being a very challenging day and 10 being one of the best, rate your day. Then complete the following statements.

I give today a rating of _____.

The best part of today was _____.

Today I learned _____.

Journal your thoughts to the following. You may substitute or add other activities if you wish.

Imagine you are a scientist who has found the cure for something. What would you cure? Describe how you would use your discovery. How would the world be different? Reflect on how you would be different if you had made this discovery. Respond on the journal page(s).

Repeat the following affirmation to yourself, *"I make a difference."*

Slowly say the first word. Pause. Say the next word, pause, and continue until you have completed the statement. Repeat the process at least 10 times. Say it to yourself or write the affirmation on the journal pages until it feels real and you believe what it says. You may want to repeat this affirmation over the following days or weeks.

THANK YOU

for being someone a child
will remember as an adult.

Most adults can remember one or more teachers who
influenced them. Perhaps a teacher said something
insightful that increased one's confidence. Or, on the
other hand, a teacher may have publicly humiliated a
student who as an adult continues to feel shame each
time the event is remembered. Like it or not, teachers
have the power to create memories that last a lifetime.
Effective teachers know this and use their power to
empower, rather than cause harm. Many times teachers
don't ever see the influences they have on students.
A teacher tells the story of being at a shopping mall
when he was approached by a young man. The teacher
did not immediately recognize the young man. The
young man called the teacher by name and proceeded
to introduce himself as a former student who had been
changed by advice the teacher had given years earlier.
But, the most interesting part of the story appeared as
the former student explained that the influence was
not a result of advice he had received directly from the
teacher. Instead the former student had overheard a
conversation between the teacher and another student in

the class. It was advice, concerning the lifelong benefits of a college education, given to a classmate that the student overheard and influenced him so dramatically. Thank you, Effective Teacher, for respecting your role as a powerful influence on the lives of learners.

SELF-CARE TOOLS

Get comfortable and take a deep breath. Let it out. It is your turn to relax. When you feel ready, reflect on your day. What went really well today? What do you wish you could have changed? On a scale of 1 to 10, with 1 being a very challenging day and 10 being one of the best, rate your day. Then complete the following statements.

I give today a rating of ———————————.

The best part of today was ———————————.

Today I learned ———————————.

Journal your thoughts to the following. You may substitute or add other activities if you wish.

Describe your greatest teacher(s) and what made this person special. To what extent does this person continue to influence your life? What did this person teach you about teaching? Use your journal to detail what you learned and why it is important to you.

Repeat the following affirmation to yourself, *"I create wonderful memories for students."*

Slowly say the first word. Pause. Say the next word, pause, and continue until you have completed the statement. Repeat the process at least 10 times. Say it to yourself or write the affirmation in your journal until it feels real and you believe what it says. You may want to repeat this affirmation over the following days or weeks.

Thank you

for wearing the hats of a nurse, counselor, motivational speaker, police officer, custodian, friend, judge, negotiator, and many others in your role as teacher.

Sometimes it may seem that teaching has quite a bit in common with parenting. Like parents, teachers meet the needs of children in a myriad of ways. When two children argue, the teacher takes on the role of mediator and convinces the students to compromise. If a learner skins a knee at school, it is often the teacher who wipes it clean and tells the student it will all be better. When a child wants to give up on a math problem, it is often the teacher who motivates him with a reminder that he has only a few more to do and then he will be finished. When the glue drips off the desk or a cup of water spills, it is the teacher who wipes it up. When a student shows up with a short skirt, it is the teacher who explains it is not consistent with dress code and sends her to the office. And when the class pet dies, it is the teacher who comforts and consoles. Thank you, Effective Teacher, for wearing many hats.

Self-Care Tools

Get comfortable and take a deep breath. Let it out. It is your turn to relax. When you feel ready, reflect on your day. What went really well today? What do you wish you could have changed? On a scale of 1 to 10, with 1 being a very challenging day and 10 being one of the best, rate your day. Then complete the following statements.

I give today a rating of ———————————.

The best part of today was ———————————.

Today I learned ———————————.

Journal your thoughts to the following. You may substitute or add other activities if you wish.

Soon a museum about your life will be constructed. How would you like it to look? Decide if it would have one or more stories, windows or gardens, one room or many. Describe what you would like to exhibit. Would there be music or demonstrations? Consider the impressions you would like people to have after they leave. Reflect and respond in your journal.

Repeat the following affirmation to yourself, *"I am interesting in many ways."*

Slowly say the first word. Pause. Say the next word, pause, and continue until you have completed the statement. Repeat the process at least 10 times. Say it to yourself or write the affirmation in your journal until it feels real and you believe what it says. You may want to repeat this affirmation over the following days or weeks.

Day 30

Thank you

for honoring society by being a teacher.

There are many ways to honor society. Some people take care of the sick and elderly or the environment, while others put out fires or arrest criminals. Teachers honor society by preparing prosocial citizens who will have the necessary skills to maintain and improve it. What would our world be like without teachers? There would be a plethora of citizens who wouldn't know how to learn or use their learning to benefit mankind. Independent and productive thinking would be replaced by a tendency to conform and settle for the easiest path. Effective teachers are familiar with the side effects of taking the easiest path. They see firsthand the impacts of dropping out, giving up, and failing to take responsibility. But they also witness the power of knowledge and its ability to heal. They know that education can make the world a better place. Caring for children and helping them to achieve their full potential to benefit themselves and others is how teachers honor society. Thank you, Effective Teacher, for honoring society.

SELF-CARE TOOLS

Get comfortable and take a deep breath. Let it out. It is your turn to relax. When you feel ready, reflect on your day. What went really well today? What do you wish you could have changed? On a scale of 1 to 10, with 1 being a very challenging day and 10 being one of the best, rate your day. Then complete the following statements.

I give today a rating of ⸻.

The best part of today was ⸻.

Today I learned ⸻.

Journal your thoughts to the following. You may substitute or add other activities if you wish.

Pretend you could move in time. Consider if you would like to move forward or backward in time. For example, would you move back a few weeks or move forward several years? Decide where you would go and how long you would stay. Identify any major events you would like to experience. Would you want anyone to go with you? Reflect in your journal.

Repeat the following affirmation to yourself, *"I am extraordinary."*

Slowly say the first word. Pause. Say the next word, pause, and continue until you have completed the statement. Repeat the process at least 10 times. Say it to yourself or write the affirmation in your journal until it feels real and you believe what it says. You may want to repeat this affirmation over the following days or weeks.

CLOSING

We are nearing an end to our journey. This next activity should be fun. It involves the completion of a list of personal statements. Each statement should be read and finished with a minimal amount of effort. Please write your responses without thinking too much about them and without any judgment concerning their quality. You are the only one who will read your work, unless you decide to share it with someone. So let loose, and express yourself.

DAY 31

I love . . .
I will . . .
I want to . . .

A good day is one . . .
I have lots of . . .
I really love to . . .
I believe . . .
When I get tired . . .
I prefer . . .
I plan . . .

I am very good at . . .
I know . . .
When I feel sad . . .
I enjoy . . .
I was surprised . . .

I would be disappointed . . .
I wish . . .
When I get frustrated . . .

I would like more time to . . .
I believe in . . .
I will never . . .

I would be shocked if . . .
I dream about . . .
When I get embarrassed . . .

For me, success is . . .

I would be very surprised if . . .
I would like to talk to . . .
I can . . .

I am known as . . .

A good day is one that . . .
I remember . . .
I spend a lot of time . . .
When I am happy . . .
I would be relieved . . .
I am proudest . . .
There are times I . . .
Others know I . . .
I would like to learn . . .
I hope . . .
I admire . . .

I think about . . .

To make myself happy . . .
When I get excited . . .
A perfect moment is one that . . .
I was successful when . . .
When I am proud I . . .
Tomorrow . . .
Someday . . .

Day 31

Finale

Now that your statements are complete, it is time to participate in the final activity of this journey. Carefully review the statements you have finished. Look for themes or commonalities across your responses. Identify any specific subjects or perceptions that repeatedly appear. Is there a mood or personality to your statements? What seems particularly important? Pretend the responses were written by a stranger. What would you notice about the person who completed these statements? Consider your impression of this person. Reflect on the work.

After reviewing your completed statements, take a look through the tasks you have finished over the preceding days. Do you see the same theme appear? Notice any patterns in the responses that draw your attention. What is your impression of the "you" articulated on these pages?

Lastly, consider what you have learned about yourself in the completion of this journey. *How can this information be used to improve even further your effectiveness as a teacher and as a loving person?*

Use your journal to reflect, respond, and close.

I hope you enjoyed yourself and that you understand how much you are appreciated.

Good luck to you.

Mindy

About The Author

Mindy Jo Sloan is an artist and writer. Her academic background includes graduate degrees in school psychology. She has lived in various parts of the United States and enjoys traveling. Mindy seeks to be a lifelong learner who takes advantage of the teachings that come her way.